Four Philosophies that Shape the Middle School

by
John W. Dougherty

Library of Congress Catalog Card Number 97-65148
ISBN 0-87367-610-6
Copyright © 1997 by the Phi Delta Kappa Educational Foundation
Bloomington, Indiana

Table of Contents

Introduction

Four philosophical movements undergird the tenets of middle-level education: invitational education, democratic schools, constructivist teaching, and reflective teaching. These movements are complementary, and they offer middle-level educators ways of thinking about and implementing a comprehensive middle-level education philosophy.

Since 1963, when William M. Alexander fathered the middle school, there has been a general understanding about what should constitute a middle school and the philosophy for that institution. Alexander noted that there were four attributes of the junior high school that should continue as part of the middle school. These were: 1) a transition school between the elementary grades and the high schools, 2) a program especially adapted to meet the needs of preadolescent and early adolescent pupils, 3) a program of exploratory experiences, and 4) continued general education with a new emphasis on intellectual development.

Alexander went on to offer three new characteristics for the middle school: 1) a place where a student can get all the attention he needs from an adult who knows him well and respects his individuality, 2) a flexible curriculum and a climate in which students develop a desire for learning, and 3) school activities designed for the development of values (Alexander 1965).

Alexander and George (1981) listed 12 essential characteristics of exemplary middle schools:

- A statement of philosophy and school goals that is based on knowledge of the educational needs of boys and girls of middle school age and is used in school program planning and evaluation.
- A system for school planning and evaluation that is specifically designed for the middle school level and that involves all concerned in the school community.
- A curriculum plan for the middle school population that provides for their continuous progress, basic learning skills, use of organized knowledge, personal development activities, and other curriculum goals as locally determined.
- A program of guidance that ensures the availability of help for each student from a faculty member well known to the student.
- An interdisciplinary teacher organization that provides for team planning, teaching, and evaluation and for appropriate interdisciplinary units.
- Use of methods of student grouping for instruction that facilitate multi-age and other instructional arrangements to maximize continuous progress.
- Block scheduling and other time arrangements to facilitate flexible and efficient use of time.

- Planning and use of physical facilities to provide the flexible and varied program required for middle-schoolers.
- Instruction that uses a balanced variety of effective strategies and techniques to achieve continuous progress of each learner toward appropriate instructional objectives.
- Appropriate roles for the various individuals and groups required for continued and dynamic leadership in the middle school, with a continuing program of staff development and renewal focused on the unique problems of middle school personnel.
- A plan for evaluation of student progress and of the school itself to ensure the achievement of the goals for the school.
- Participation with other schools and with community groups in the continuing study of the middle school population and of society as a whole, to be responsible to changing needs and conditions of the future.

Echoing these characteristics was the Carnegie Task Force (1989), which called for middle schools that:

- Create small communities for learning where stable, close, mutually respectful relationships with adults and peers are considered fundamental for intellectual and personal growth.
- Teach a core academic program that results in students who are literate, including in the sciences, and who know how to think critically, lead a healthy life, behave ethically, and assume the responsibili-

ties of citizenship in a pluralistic society. Youth service to promote values for citizenship is an essential part of the core academic program.

- Ensure success for all students through elimination of tracking by achievement level and promotion of cooperative learning, flexibility in arranging instructional time, and adequate resources for teachers.
- Empower teachers and administrators to make decisions about the experiences of middle-grade students through creative control by teachers of the instructional program linked to greater responsibilities for students' performances, governance committees that assist the principal in designing and coordinating schoolwide programs, and autonomy and leadership within subschools or houses to create environments tailored to enhance the intellectual and emotional development of all youth.
- Staff middle-grade schools with teachers who are expert at teaching young adolescents and who have been specially prepared for assignment to the middle grades.
- Improve academic performance through fostering the health and fitness of young adolescents.
- Re-engage families in the education of young adolescents by giving families meaningful roles in school governance, communicating with families about the school program and student's progress, and offering families opportunities to support the learning process at home and at the school.
- Connect schools with communities, which together share responsibility for each middle-grade

student's success, through identifying service opportunities in the community, establishing partnerships and collaborations to ensure students' access to health and social services, and using community resources to enrich the instructional program and opportunities for constructive after-school activities.

Thus middle schools were and are guided by the concept of function. Gruhn and Douglass (1956) summarized these functions as: integration, exploration, guidance, differentiation, socialization, and articulation. Middle schools create small, personalized communities for learning; emphasize a strong academic core curriculum; address the individual needs of the learner; emphasize the importance of physical and emotional health in achieving academic excellence and personal development; decentralize the decision-making process; have teachers who are experts in teaching the young adolescent, rather than experts in teaching subject matter; engage families in the education of their children; and connect communities to the school.

As middle-level educators guide their schools in fulfilling these functions, it behooves them to implement the philosophies of invitational education and democratic principles, as well as constructivist and reflective instruction.

Invitational Education

Crystal Kuykendall, in *From Rage to Hope*, wrote: "An effective teacher can give a child hope. With hope, there is reason to look to tomorrow. Without hope, life is meaningless. Without hope, there is greater propensity for negative behavior" (1992, p. xv).

Education is a profession of hope. This hope generates an educational vision and suggests creative means of attainment. Without hope, individuals become mere technicians and functionaries in a bureaucratic system. Without vision and the responsibility to attain that vision, educators can become functional robots. The components of middle schools do indeed become the functions needed to change schools into institutions of hope, into inviting schools.

Definition

Our English word *invite* probably is a derivative of the Latin word *invitare*, which can mean "to offer something beneficial for consideration." Translated literally it means "to summon cordially, not to shun." The word *education* also comes from the Latin and means "to draw out" or "call forth" (Purkey and Novak 1984). Thus invitational education is the process by which people are cordially summoned to realize their potential in all areas of worthwhile human endeavor. *Potential* refers to those innate abilities of people that can be connected to worthwhile opportunities that encourage refinement and future possibilities for growth. It is within the 10- to 14-year-old age range that students discover that they have *potential*.

Invitational education redirects the energy of current challenges to schooling by reconnecting with the hopes of educators, by heading educational practices in a defensible and consistent direction, and by offering strategies for handling difficult situations. To do this, educators must work from a language that expresses care (Purkey and Novak 1984). Caring is reflected through modeling, dialogue, practice, and confirmation (Noddings 1986).

Philosophy

Invitational education is a general framework for thinking (reflecting) about and acting on what is believed to be worthwhile in democratic schools. Democratically oriented, perceptually anchored, and with a self-concept approach to the educational process, invitational education centers on five basic principles:

1. People are able, valuable, and responsible and should be treated accordingly.
2. Educating should be a collaborative, cooperative activity.
3. The process is the product in the making.
4. People possess untapped potential in all areas of worthwhile human endeavor.

5. This potential can best be realized by places, policies, programs, and processes specifically designed to invite development and by people who are intentionally inviting with themselves and others, both personally and professionally (Purkey and Novak 1984).

In *How We Think*, John Dewey said, "Everything the teacher does as well as the manner in which he does it incites the child to respond in some way or another and each response tends to set the child's attitude in some way or another" (1933, p. 59). William James stated: "No more fiendish punishment could be devised, were such a thing possible, than that one should be turned loose in society and remain absolutely unnoticed by all the members thereof" (1890, p.179). Martin Buber added, "Man wishes to be confirmed in his being man, and wishes to have a presence in the being of others. . . . secretly and bashfully he watches for a Yes which allows him to be and which can come only from one human person to another. It is from one person to another that the heavenly bread of self-being is passed" (1965, p. 71). Each of the these statements is an endorsement for inviting schools.

Rather than viewing people as objects to be shaped, reinforced, and conditioned, or as captives of subconscious urges or unfilled desires, this tradition views people as they typically see themselves, others, and the world (Purkey and Novak 1984). This is in keeping with the middle school belief that part of the school's goal is to assist adolescents in understanding themselves. (See

14

fastback 268 *Education: By Invitation Only* by William W. Purkey and John M. Novak.)

Invitational education is based on an understanding of, and respect for, people's perceptual worlds. Perceptions serve as a reference point for behavior. Perception determines how people see themselves and the situations in which they are involved and how they behave accordingly. Gerler notes:

> In their struggle for identity, many adolescents come to view themselves as creatures apart from humanity, alienated from the mainstream. They perpetuate such thoughts as "no one feels the way I do about anything — my problems are larger than life, unlike those of anyone else" and "no one cares about me." In short, the search for identity, one of the principal tasks of adolescence, leaves many young people feeling alone and without hope. (1986, p. 63)

Human behavior is motivated by self-perception. For example, alcohol consumption appears to be used by social drinkers and alcoholics alike to reduce perceptions of personal failure. Clarity can be quite painful at times (Hull and Young 1993). Students who view themselves as troublemakers may respond by being discipline problems. Others who view themselves as scholars may spend hours in the libraries. Behavior reflects personality.

The ingredients of self-concept are primarily social, obtained through countless interactions with persons, places, policies, programs, and processes. As a way of interpreting oneself, each individual attaches meaning to the acts of others. It is a belief of "I am who I am because of the manner in which others treat me, or the way I perceive others treating me."

In similar fashion, Patterson says, "The concepts which the teacher has of the children become the concepts which the children come to have of themselves" (1973, p. 125). The effects of teachers' expectations on the achievement of students has been well documented. Each teacher's task, therefore, is to behave in ways that encourage positive perceptions in students regarding themselves and their abilities (Purkey and Novak 1984). Substantial evidence can be found of a relationship between young adolescents' perceptions of the classroom environment and their achievement and attitudes. Nurturing teachers, high levels of student involvement, participation, and decision making are all important in the education of young people; and all of these are reflected in middle schools.

Implementation

Alice could be the quintessential middle-schooler. In Lewis Carroll's *Alice in Wonderland*, she exclaims, "Dear, dear! How queer everything is today! And yesterday things went on just as usual. I wonder if I've been changed in the night? Let me think: Was I the same when I got up this morning? I almost think I can remember feeling a little different. But if I'm not the same, the next question is 'Who in the World am I?' Ah, that's the puzzle!"

Middle school students wake up every day not really sure of who they are. Sometimes they will play with Barbie dolls or trucks with the fourth-grader up the street; on other days they will discuss fashions or cars with the sophomore next door. Early adolescence is a time of not quite giving up the past and not quite embracing the future.

The process of growing up is the process of trying things out, of making mistakes, and of finding successes (Beane and Lipka 1987). Helping students in this process is one of the goals of an effective advisory program in the middle schools, often termed an "advisor/advisee" program. Such programs are based on the premise that kids should come first and that school should be an exciting place where adolescents can discover who they are and how they fit into a bewildering world. Connors says:

> Hopefully, through advisory sessions, students can meet with caring, sensitive, and informed adults who are prepared to help students learn how to make decisions and deal with their own personal development and self-concept. (1992, p. 163)

For middle-level educators, the advisory program is a means of expressing care. A caring — inviting — message is a summary description of those communications, which are transmitted by people, places, policies, programs, or processes.

But middle schools become inviting schools through the use of two institutional components: advisory programs *and* interdisciplinary teaming. These two aspects of middle-level education are most effective when staffed by middle school teachers who care. When they are so staffed, then the caring aspect of invitational education adds even more effectiveness to these essentially middle school concepts. Epstein and MacIver state:

> The aim [of interdisciplinary teaming] is to minimize the number of students who feel that no teacher knows them, that the teachers do not know how they are doing in other classes, or that no students know them well enough to accept them as friends. . . . Interdisciplinary teaming helps students build team spirit and improves attitudes and work habits because of the closer, more coherent supervision and caring that occurs on a team. (1990, p. 34)

The interdisciplinary teaming concept at the middle level sends an inviting message to the young adolescents. Hawkins and Berndt (1985) state that there is evidence to show that breaking large schools into smaller units contributes to students' feelings of being well known, liked, and supported.

Democratic Schools

Perhaps through invitational education a now half-forgotten idea that was to guide the programs of our public schools will be remembered. The idea was, and is, democracy.

Democratic practices are the guiding ideals that focus on developing continuous dialogue and mutual respect among people regarding shared aspects of their lives. A commitment to democratic practice is therefore a commitment to the conditions and processes that make mutual respect and continuous dialogue possible. These conditions and processes also are essential to invitational education.

In a democratic social order, one hopes that the educational process will enable all involved to participate in continual self-realization and in the self-rule of their society. Inviting schools summon everyone to be participants; and so, too, must democratic schools. In *Democracy and Education*, John Dewey wrote:

> A society which makes provisions for participation in its good of all its members on equal terms and which secures flexible readjustment of its institutions through interaction of the different forms of associated life is in so far democratic. Such a society must have a type of

education which gives individuals a personal interest in social relationships and control, and the habits of the mind which secure social changes without introducing disorder. (1916, p. 90)

In addition to participation, democracy requires excellence in education for all. Ten- to fourteen-year-old adolescents first become aware of the world and the democratic process in the middle school. Prior to this age, they are primarily self-centered and their "world view" is much narrower. The authors of *An Imperiled Generation: Saving Urban Schools* (Carnegie Foundation 1988) state:

Without good schools none of America's hopes can be fulfilled. The quality of our education will determine the strength of our democracy, the vitality of our economy, and the promise of our ideals. It is through schools that this nation has chosen to pursue enlightened ends for all its people. And it is here that the battle for the future of America will be won or lost. (p. xi)

Definition

Where the family is the primary socialization agent at a personal level, the school serves as a socialization agent at a societal level. The school, more than the family, prepares young people for participation in a democracy. It prepares young people to enter the work force; it prepares young people to interact with other people; and it prepares young people to appreciate and transmit the traditions and values inherent in the society. The public school is more than an institution concerned with the transmission of cognitive knowledge. It is a social institution whose core values are concerned with developing citizens who will support and reinforce dominant civic and ethical values (Sinclair and Finn 1989).

Dewey said, "A democracy is more than a form of government; it is primarily a mode of associated living, of conjoint communicated experiences" (1916, p. 87). Democracy is the central tenet of our social and political relations. It is the basis for how we govern ourselves, the concept by which we measure the wisdom and worth of social policies and shifts, and the ethical anchor we seek when our political ship seems to drift (Apple and Beane 1995). Middle school students learn these things as they interact with one another and with their teachers and as they observe adult interactions.

Communities of learners in democratic schools are marked by an emphasis on cooperation and collaboration (Apple and Beane 1995). These are the same beliefs that spawned the middle school movement, with emphasis on collaboration through teaming and cooperative learning.

Philosophy

The school's major function is to perpetuate the values and traditions inherent in a democratic society that is composed of free people who have each other's interests in mind. The democratic way of life depends on conditions that are the central concerns of democratic schools:

- The open flow of ideas, regardless of their popularity, that enables people to be as fully informed as possible.

- Faith in the individual and collective capacity of people to create possibilities for resolving problems.
- The use of critical reflection and analysis to evaluate ideas, problems, and policies.
- Concern for the welfare of others and the "common good."
- Concern for the dignity and rights of individuals and minorities.
- An understanding that democracy is not so much an "ideal" to be pursued as an "idealized" set of values that we must live and that must guide our life as a people.
- The organization of social institutions to promote and extend the democratic way of life (Apple and Beane 1995).

Many people believe that democracy is nothing more than a form of federal government and thus does not apply to schools and other social institutions. Many believe that democracy is a right of adults, not of young people (Apple and Beane 1995). In fact, the effective middle school provides opportunities for young people to practice the tenets of democracy. It is a place where their voices may and should be heard. "Surely, it is an obligation of education in a democracy to empower the young to become members of the public, to participate, and play articulate roles in the public space" (Greene 1985, p. 4).

A school cannot teach students ethical values and the meaning of participation in a democratic society only by the teaching of civic and ethical principles. The school community must live these principles and infuse them into the school's culture. These principles are several. According to Calabrese (1990), schools are places of integrity:

- where justice prevails;
- where equity is cherished;
- that expect full participation;
- where inclusion is practiced;
- that distribute resources equitably; and
- that allow members resources to redress grievances.

The authors of *Turning Points* state:

Caring is crucial to the development of young adolescents into healthy adults. Young adolescents need to see themselves as valued members of a group that offers mutual support and trusting relationships. They need to be able to succeed at something, and to be praised and rewarded for that success. They need to become socially competent individuals who have the skills to cope successfully with the exigencies of everyday life. They need to believe that they have a promising future, and they need the competence to take advantage of real opportunities in a society in which they have a stake. (Carnegie Task Force 1989, p. 33)

A government, a society, or an institution cannot re-establish itself for each generation. The ancestors of the inheritors must pass on the organization's or institution's basic beliefs, traditions, and workings to the next generation. Mursell commented:

If the schools of a democratic society do not exist for and work for the support and extension of democracy, they are either socially useless or socially dangerous. At the best they will educate people who will go their way and earn their living indifferent to the obligations of citizenship in particular and of the democratic way of life in general. . . . But quite likely they will educate people to be enemies of democracy — people who will fall prey to demagogues, and who back movements and rally round leaders hostile to the democratic way of life. Such schools are either futile or subversive. They have no legitimate reason for existence. (1955, p. 3)

Implementation

If people are to secure and maintain a democratic way of life, they must have opportunities to learn what that way of life means and how it might be led (Dewey 1916). Middle schools, through interdisciplinary teaming and advisory programs, provide the opportunities for adolescents to be members of a productive, functional, contributing social organization that is supported by the larger social order. In the case of the middle school, the team is supported not only by the larger school itself but also by the community that supports the school and the district. Membership depends on social bonding, the extent to which an individual forms meaningful and satisfying links with a social group and the extent to which the group encourages the formation of these bonds (Hirschi 1969).

Democratic schools are meant to be democratic places, and so the idea of democracy also extends to the many roles that adults play in the schools (Apple and Beane 1995). Middle schools embrace the involvement of parents. Opportunities to interact with a team of teachers and through each student's advisor means that parents more often become involved in the school community than when they had to communicate individually with six or seven teachers in traditional junior high school.

To say that democracy rests on the consent of the governed is almost a cliché; but in a democratic school it is true that all of those directly involved in the school, including the students, must have the right to participate in making decisions. Young people and teachers engage in collaborative planning, reaching decisions that respond to the concerns, aspirations, and interests of both (Apple and Beane 1995).

Dewey maintained that the school should be run as miniature society. Democracy is basically the attempt to find the right practical integration of what we described as the fundamental values of political or group life — liberty, equality, and cooperation, or fraternity. Participation in this miniature society should foster an appreciation of liberty that is not viewed just as individualism, of equality that gives opportunity and scope for the development of valuable personal talents, and of cooperation that does not mean mere conformism.

Through teaming and block scheduling, middle school teachers have become empowered to make decisions concerning what is best for their students. Democratic educators seek not simply to lessen the harshness of social inequities in school but to change the conditions that create them (Apple and Beane 1995). Thus tracking is not a part of the middle school philosophy. Interdisciplinary teaming provides for meeting individual student needs.

Educators who care about democracy also must stand firm against racism, injustice, centralized power, poverty, and other inequities in school and society. Through service learning, middle-level students are given opportunities to observe and correct some social injustices and to improve their communities. Such activities foster cooperation that it is directed at the solution of a shared or group problem, with each member of the group making a contribution to the solution of the common problem.

In a democratic society, no individual or interest group can claim sole ownership of knowledge and meaning. Likewise, a democratic curriculum includes not only what adults think is important but also the questions and concerns that young people have about themselves and their world. James A. Beane suggests that "curriculum themes should emerge from the natural overlaps between the personal concerns of early adolescents and the larger issues that face our world. In the intersections between these two categories, we may discover a promising way to conceptualizing a general education that serves the dual purpose of addressing the personal issues, needs, and problems of the early adolescents and the concerns of the larger world, including the particular society in which they live" (Beane 1990). This approach is often tried in developing interdisciplinary units at the middle school level.

A democratic curriculum invites young people to shed the passive role of "knowledge consumer" and to adopt the active role of "meaning maker." It also recognizes that young people acquire knowledge both by studying external sources and by engaging in complex activities that require them to construct their own knowledge. For example, the school can introduce students to the rule of law. Schools, like society, are structured associations that impose limits on individual freedom in order to function smoothly. Thus they operate under definite rules and regulations. If the students are involved in the drawing up of these rules and regulations, then they learn one democratic principle: government by the people.

Regardless of how much participation teachers enjoy in determining the school program, true democracy in the school has not been attained until the students are given the opportunity to participate in the plans and conduct of those activities that concern them (Bolmeier 1947).

Constructivist Teaching

Each individual constructs an understanding of the world in which he or she lives. Each makes sense of the world by synthesizing new experiences with existing understandings. Teachers must provide a learning environment in which students search for meaning, appreciate uncertainty, and inquire responsibly (Brooks and Brooks 1993). In other words, they should provide experiences from which the learner can *construct* meaning.

In *Science of Education and the Psychology of the Child*, Jean Piaget wrote:

> If the aim of intellectual training is to form intelligence rather than to stock the memory, and to produce intellectual explorers rather than mere erudition, then traditional education is manifestly guilty of a grave deficiency. (1970, pp. 149-50)

Piaget explained that children gain knowledge by constructing it. He believed that knowledge is not a state that children are in, but rather a process in which they are engaged. Children learn by inventing. They need to be actively engaged in seeking solutions to problems and answers to questions.

Definition

Constructivism is not a theory about teaching but one about knowledge and learning. Knowledge is temporary, developmental, socially and culturally mediated, and thus non-objective. Learning is a self-regulated process of resolving inner cognitive conflicts that often become apparent through concrete experiences, collaborative discourse, and reflection. Educators must begin to make a difference in how students learn by encouraging student-to-student interaction, initiating lessons that foster cooperative learning, and providing interdisciplinary curricula (Brooks and Brooks 1993).

Piaget viewed constructivism as a way of explaining how people come to view the world. He suggested that cognitive functioning involves the complementary processes of assimilation and accommodation. Assimilation is a shaping process in which new experiences are received though existing knowledge structures, while accommodation is *reshaping* the existing knowledge structures to accept the new experience. That is, new things are understood in relation to existing knowledge; but the new experiences also reshape the old knowledge. Piaget summed it up by stating, "Knowledge comes neither from the subject nor the object, but from the unity of the two" (1971, p. 158).

Philosophy

Following are basic understandings of constructivist teaching. (Readers also may wish to consult fastback 390 *Constructivist Teaching* by John A. Zahorik.)

- Knowledge is actively created or invented by the child, not passively received from the environment.
- Ideas are constructed when children integrate them into their existing knowledge structures.
- Learning is a social process in which children grow into a shared intellectual life with those around them. The constructivist classroom is seen not only as a culture in which children are involved in invention, but also as the setting of a social discourse involving explanations, negotiations, and sharing.

Knowledge is not a set of facts, concepts, or laws waiting to be discovered. It does not exist without the knower. Humans create knowledge as they attempt to make sense out of their experiences. Their understanding becomes deeper and stronger as it is tested against new experiences (Zahorik 1995). In constructivist teaching, individuals are seen as questioners, explorers, problem solvers, and concept creators (Poplin 1988).

Individuals also construct knowledge within the social context in which they find themselves. Developmental psychologists stress that the cognitive or intellectual development of an individual cannot be separated from the social context surrounding the person. Not only does individual growth and development take place with social support, but the tools of thought developed by the culture mediate individual activity. Different cultures construct forms of knowledge, ways of thinking, values, and perspectives on the world to fit their own physical and social circumstances.

Implementation

Because real comprehension involves reinvention by the student, the teacher should be less an assigner of lessons and more an organizer of engaging problems.

Many students struggle to understand concepts in isolation, to learn parts without seeing the whole, to make connections where they see only disparity, and to accept as reality what their perceptions question. Often, students' success in school is not a measure of their understanding but merely of how much of the curriculum they have covered (Brooks and Brooks 1993). This is the old junior high model, wherein learning was seen as a "mimetic" activity.

Constructivist teaching helps learners to internalize and to reshape information — in other words, to reinvent their knowledge. Such reinvention occurs through the creation of new understandings. Because the knowledge structure in its entirety will be used to perceive new information, the teacher needs to focus on wholes and to assist the student in acquiring them. To develop understanding, students need to see the "big picture," as well as its various parts. Isolated bits of content do not permit the understanding needed to add to the knowledge structure. Understanding comes not from the quantity of information covered, but rather from the depth of material, which activates the entire knowledge structure.

Focusing on wholes means identifying a few major ideas and making them the center of instruction. Thematic units and interdisciplinary units in the middle school are examples of focusing on the whole by all of the teachers instructing a child. In addition, the teaming component and school-within-a-school organization of middle schools extend that "whole" to the social setting and the community of learners.

Reflective Teaching

As students construct their understandings and add to their knowledge structures, so, too, do teachers construct their understanding of the processes of teaching and learning. Teachers can use their experiences to examine their beliefs about teaching. Beliefs and behaviors are reciprocal; a critical examination of our beliefs encourages us to rethink our actions. This process may be called reflection, and the teaching that grows from this process is rightly termed reflective teaching.

Deborah P. Britzman, in *Practice Makes Practice: A Critical Study of Learning to Teach*, comments:

> Learning to teach — like teaching itself — is always the process of becoming; a time of formation and transformation, of scrutiny into what one is doing, and who one can become.

Humans have the remarkable potential for becoming self-aware, for being able to put problems into words, numbers, drama, art, and so forth. When faced by a problem, we reflect, we become more aware, we search for clues or hints about solutions, and we explore the consequences of our hunches. We reflect on our feelings, values, and interpersonal styles. We try to understand why students or colleagues react as they do to what we do or say. Research clearly shows that intellectual maturity is marked by reflective self-insight.

Definition

Valverde (1982) defines reflective teachers as those who review, reconstruct, re-enact, and critically analyze their own and their students' performances and who formulate explanations with evidence. Reflective teachers view themselves not as passive, but as proactive participants in curricular and instructional decisions.

Van Manen (1977) proposes three levels of reflectivity: 1) using basic technical skills (instructional skills, classroom management skills, subject matter content) to perform the art of teaching; 2) critically analyzing the rationale for the educational practices (What should be learned? What is the best way for each student to learn this material?); and 3) making connections between what happens in the classroom and the wider moral and social structures that impinge on a classroom.

In his books, *The Reflective Practitioner* (1973) and *Educating the Reflective Practitioner* (1987), Donald Schon describes two types of reflection. *Reflection-on-action* is reflection on practice and on one's actions and thoughts, undertaken after the practice is completed. *Reflection-in-action* is reflection on phenomena and on one's spontaneous ways of thinking and acting in the midst of action. A third type of reflection, *Reflection-for-action*, is the desired outcome of both previous types of reflection.

Reflection is a process that simultaneously encompasses all time designations — past, present, and future.

First, a teacher plans to act. Then through reflection-in-action, the teacher observes the action as it transpires, almost as if placing him- or herself outside the action. Finally, by engaging in reflection-on-action, the teacher analyzes events and draws conclusions that guide (reflection-for-action) future decisions.

Philosophy

Reflective teaching requires teachers to be willing to think seriously about the origins and consequences of their actions and decisions and about the situations and constraints embedded in the instructional, curricular, school, and social contexts in which they work. Teachers must consider the moral, ethical, and social complexities of teaching and must think rigorously, critically, and systematically about educational practices and problems in order to grow as professionals.

Zeichner (1983) poses the following general questions for reflective thought:

- What knowledge should be taught and to whom?
- How should a teacher allocate time and resources among different children?
- To what extent should personal knowledge that children bring to school be considered a legitimate part of the school curriculum?
- How much control do (and should) teachers exert in determining what is taught, how it is to be taught, and how it is to be evaluated?

Mature reflection can provide self-confidence, unity of purpose, and a sense of direction in the teaching role.

Reflective teachers also want their students to become reflective thinkers.

Implementation

In most school settings, particularly at the high school level and in the traditional junior high, teachers have too many students to get to know each one personally. If they are able to get to know individual students on a more personal basis, this information often is not shared with the student's other teachers. Teachers in isolation accept a role that is more technical than professional, more immediately responsive than reflective, and more individualistic than participatory. By contrast, middle school teaming encourages and supports teacher reflection as a group process.

Dewey said, "Experience + Reflection = Growth." According to Dewey, reflective teaching requires a teacher to "turn a subject over in the mind and give it serious and consecutive consideration" (1933, p. 40). Teachers change more readily as a consequence of interacting with one another around common problems than when they are told to change by administrators or "experts" (Bentzen 1975).

In the middle schools, teachers more often have the responsibility to make decisions concerning the scheduling of class time in individual subjects, which students will be in which subjects with whom, and various kinds of team experiences. Schon (1987) asserts that although teachers gain some professional knowledge from traditional principles and skills, the bulk of their learning comes from continuous action and reflection on everyday problems. Meaningful dialogue with other professional colleagues enhances reflection. This dialogue is more beneficial with those who are involved in the same arena of performance. In the middle school, this arena is the interdisciplinary team.

Reflection is not a brief mental replay of a series of events. Busy people typically do not engage in reflection. They rarely treat themselves to reflective experiences, unless they are given some time, some structure, and the expectation to do so. The team planning time, so prevalent in many middle schools, offers the teaching team the opportunity to be reflective as a group and individually.

District and state curriculum guides have tried to stipulate what should be taught and at what grade level. This assumes prior knowledge is the same for all students and there is a common pre-existing knowledge structure. Obviously, this cannot be the case. Through the interdisciplinary process in the middle school, teachers are expected to make decisions about what should be taught based on the actual knowledge of real students. Teams of teachers can gain closer knowledge of students because they have the advantage of multiple, shared perspectives on each student. They can use this shared information to plan a more tailored, relevant curriculum. Most middle schools provide block schedules so that instructional time can be allocated to specific subjects by the teachers on the team. The team teachers also may group children and allocate resources based on individual student needs. By using thematic units in interdisciplinary teams, middle school teachers also can control the education setting.

The more a teacher understands the student, the better the insight into the knowledge structures of the student and hence the experiences that are likely to enable the student to connect new information to existing information. The reflection process encourages this to happen. One of the great advantages of team teaching is that it provides an arena where great energy and dynamic interplay go into hammering out a philosophy with which its creators can live comfortably and draw support for their collective efforts. Teaching has too often been called a "lonely" profession, but it need not be so.

Conclusion

When one receives an invitation, it is generally to an occasion of joy, a celebration, an opportunity to be with people one likes. Inviting schools are those that promise participants a rewarding time. Middle schools invite students to become a part of an exciting group of people — a team. The students will have someone to guide them through the difficult parts and to help them celebrate the good parts.

Middle school should be an invitation to a "gentle education" — one that is gentle on the mind and the emotions and one that is free of school-induced stress. Adolescence is stressful enough by itself. Students should feel this gentleness as they enter the school and always remember middle school with fondness in later years. Gentleness is fostered by caring teachers.

Teacher caring is the single most important prerequisite to student success in middle school. In and of itself, caring is responsible for improved self-esteem among students; and improved self-esteem is a key ingredient to getting kids to work harder and last longer in school. There also is a structural effect of teacher caring. The caring teacher is always thinking of ways to improve the performance of the school and the lives of students. Bureaucratic roadblocks to implementing caring teachers' work need to be removed (Benedict 1992).

If the effective middle school, through its teaming and advisor-advisee components, invites children to a gentle education, then it is complemented by teacher education programs that prepare teachers to teach and to treat young adolescents differently than they would have been treated in the junior high. It often is said that there is no in-between with middle-level children: One either likes them or doesn't. Period. And the students know if teachers do not really like them. Thus the middle school philosophy has yet another component: Middle school teachers must like this age group or they will not be successful at teaching them. This, too, is a component of teacher education — discovering those teachers best suited to teach young adolescents and nurturing that match.

Caring teachers who want their students to learn and are concerned about *how* they learn usually embrace constructivism. Teaming in the middle school is structured around the concept of helping students connect all of their educational experiences. Teaming and presenting thematic and interdisciplinary units enable young adolescents to construct and add to their knowledge. Elementary teachers have been doing this kind of interdisciplinary, "whole child" work for many years. The effective middle school adopts and extends this aspect of the elementary school years.

Constructivist teachers also are adept at helping students connect their classroom experiences to the real world. Combined with interdisciplinary teams and advisory programs, these connections help the middle school to foster democratic ideals among students. In its broadest sense, constructivist teaching (interdisciplinary teaching) is designed to help students to "see life whole," to integrate and make sense out of the myriad experiences they have, both in school and in the world (Vars 1993).

A "curriculum" developed apart from the teachers and young people who must live it is grossly undemocratic, because such a curriculum deprives both students and teachers of their right to have a say in their own lives and to learn and apply the skills and understandings associated with making important decisions (Beane 1990, p. 16). The middle school curriculum should be conceived democratically through collaborative planning with the involvement of students. The voices of teachers are not meant to be silenced by this strategy, but neither are they to be the dominant authority. The key concept is "collaboration," the building of communities in which the interests of all people, adults and the young, are sources of curriculum.

Furthermore, in a democratic curriculum, information or "facts" brought into the classroom should be open to critical analysis, rather than presented for passive assimilation (Beane 1990).

Mills (1956) wrote that the individual is an agent of the transformation of society and must become aware of and participate in the public issues of the day. Men and women are both creators and creations of society; they must be made conscious of the human condition.

They must become active agents in society, rather than mere spectators.

The transmission of culture and the continuation of a society is the primary task of the education system. The values, beliefs, and norms of a society are maintained and passed to the next generation not merely by teaching about them, but also by the embodiment of these cultural elements in the operation of the education system. Democratic education will produce men and women who have the tastes, knowledge, and character supportive of a democracy.

Finally, education is a moral enterprise. Schooling transmits values, as well as skills, in three dimensions: study, example, and practice. *Study* is disciplined inquiry and work. It is what teachers assign and tests measure. Sometimes, it may not be much fun; but when study is successful, it is most rewarding. *Example* convinces students that study and learning are both worth doing and worth doing well. Teachers are, or should be, role models, men and women of integrity and dedication. Through example, they inspire. Last, *practice* — learning by doing, trial and error, experimentation, and diligence — is important. It is both the basis for service to family, community, and state and the foundation of the scientific method for modern society.

The philosophical movements of invitational education, democratic schools, constructivist teaching, and reflective teaching are complementary. Converging in the middle school, they provide a sound basis for educators to provide meaningful learning experiences for young adolescents.

References

Alexander, William M. "The Junior High School: A Changing View." In *Readings in Curriculum*, edited by G. Hass and K. Wiles. Boston: Allyn & Bacon, 1965.

Alexander, A.M., and George, P.S. *The Exemplary Middle School*. New York: Holt, Rinehart and Winston, 1981.

Apple, M.W., and Beane, J.A. *Democratic Schools*. Alexandria, Va.: Association for Supervision and Curriculum Development, 1995.

Beane, James A. *A Middle School Curriculum: From Rhetoric to Reality*. Columbus, Ohio: National Middle School Association, 1990.

Beane, J., and Lipka, R. *When the Kids Come First: Enhancing Self-Esteem*. Columbus, Ohio: National Middle School Association, 1987.

Benedict, R. *Trashcan Kids*. Alexandria, Va.: Association for Supervision and Curriculum Development, 1992.

Bentzen, M.M. *Changing Schools: The Magic Feather Principle*. New York: McGraw-Hill, 1975.

Bolmeier, E.C. "6 Steps to Pupil Participation in Democratic School Control." *Clearing House* 21 (March 1947).

Britzman, D. *Practice Makes Practice: A Critical Study of Learning to Teach*. Albany: State University of New York Press, 1991.

Brooks, J.G., and Brooks, M.G. *In Search of Understanding: The Case for Constructivist Classrooms*. Alexandria, Va.: Association for Supervision and Curriculum Development, 1993.

Buber, M. *The Knowledge of Man: Selected Essays*. New York: Harper & Row, 1965.

Calabrese, R.L. "The School as an Ethical and Democratic Community." *NASSP Bulletin* (October 1990): 10-15.

Carnegie Foundation for the Advancement of Teaching. *An Imperiled Generation: Saving Urban Schools*. Washington, D.C.: Carnegie Council on Adolescent Development, 1988.

Carnegie Task Force on Education of Young Adolescents. *Turning Points: Preparing American Youth for the 21st Century*. Washington, D.C.: Carnegie Council on Adolescent Development, 1989.

Connors, N.A. "Teacher Advisory: The Fourth R." In *Transforming Middle Level Education. Perspectives and Possibilities*, edited by Judith I. Irvin. Needham Heights, Mass.: Allyn & Bacon, 1992.

Dewey, J. *Democracy and Education*. New York: Macmillan, 1916.

Dewey, J. *How We Think*. Lexington, Mass.: D.C. Heath, 1933.

Epstein, J.L., and MacIver, D.J. *Education in the Middle Grades: Overview of National Practices and Trends*. Columbus, Ohio: National Middle School Association, 1990.

Gerler, R. "Teaching Teenagers Skills for Adolescence." *Education Digest* 52, no. 2 (1986): 36-38.

Greene, M. "The Role of Education in Democracy." *Educational Horizons* 63 (Special Issue 1985): 3-9.

Gruhn, W.T., and Douglass, Harl R. *The Modern Junior High School*. New York: Ronald Press, 1956.

Hawkins, J.A., and Berndt, T.J. "Adjustment Following the Transition to Junior High School." Paper presented at the meeting of the Society for Research in Child Development, Toronto, April 1985.

Hirschi, T. *Causes of Delinquency*. Los Angeles: University of California Press, 1969.

Hull, J., and Young, R. "The Self-Awareness-Reducing Effects of Alcohol: Evidence and Implications." In *Psychological Perspectives on the Self*, vol. 2, edited by J. Suls and A. Grenwald. Hillsdale, N.J.: Lawrence Erlbaum Associates, 1993.

James, W. *Principles of Psychology*. 2 vols. New York: Henry Holt, 1890.

Kuykendall, Crystal. *From Rage to Hope: Strategies for Reclaiming Black and Hispanic Students*. Bloomington, Ind.: National Educational Service, 1992.

McIntyre, D.J., and O'Hair, M.J. *The Reflective Roles of the Classroom Teacher*. New York: Wadsworth, 1996.

Mills, C.W. *The Power Elite*. New York: Oxford University Press, 1956.

Mursell, James. *Principles of Democratic Education*. New York: Norton, 1955.

Noddings, N. "Fidelity in Teaching, Teacher Education, and Research for Teaching." *Harvard Educational Review* 54, no. 4 (1986): 496-510.

Patterson, C.H. *Humanistic Education*. Englewood Cliffs, N.J.: Prentice-Hall, 1973.

Piaget, J. *Science of Education and the Psychology of the Child*. New York: Orion, 1970.

Piaget, J. *Genetic Epistemology*. New York: Norton, 1971.

Poplin, M. "Holistic Constructivist Principles of the Teaching/Learning Process: Implications for the Field of Learning Disabilities." *Journal of Learning Disabilities* 21, no. 7 (1988): 401-16.

Purkey, W.W., and Novak, J.M. *Inviting School Success: A Self-Concept Approach to Teaching and Learning*. 2nd ed. Belmont, Calif.: Wadsworth, 1984.

Schon, D. *The Reflective Practitioner*. New York: Basic Books, 1973.

Schon, D. *Educating the Reflective Practitioner*. San Francisco: Jossey-Bass, 1987.

Sinclair, R., and Finn, B. *Matters of Consequence*. Amherst, Mass.: Coalition for School Improvement, 1989.

Valverde, L. "The Self-Evolving Supervisor." In *Supervision of Teaching*, edited by T. Sergiovanni. Alexandria, Va.: Association for Supervision and Curriculum Development, 1982.

Van Manen, M. "Linking Ways of Knowing with Ways of Being Parallel." *Curriculum Inquiry* 6 (1977): 205-28.

Vars, G.F. *Interdisciplinary Teaching*. Columbus, Ohio: National Middle School Association, 1993.

Zahorik, J.A. *Constructivist Teaching*. Fastback 390. Bloomington, Ind.: Phi Delta Kappa Educational Foundation, 1995.

Zeichner, K. "Alternative Paradigms of Teacher Education." *Journal of Teacher Education* 34, no. 3 (1983): 3-9.